Nostalgia Street
Part One

Tony Usher

Illustrated by Sandra Chapman Ford

Published by New Generation Publishing in 2022

First Edition

ISBN

      Paperback   978-1-80369-149-7
      Hardback   978-1-80369-150-3

www.newgeneration-publishing.com

New Generation Publishing

In memory of Michael and Paul Usher, and Julie O'Loughlin

Introduction

Dear reader, I was never one for social media and until 2015 I only used it to Facetime or private message my friends and family in Australia, America, Tenerife and the Middle East as it was instamatic and cost nothing. However, when my physical ailments left me housebound in 2015, I opened up my Facebook account to the general public and eventually opened my own group mainly for people with a similar upbringing to myself who had basically no interaction with the outside world After spending roughly nine months on and off in my parent's cottage/ holiday let, which had been adapted for my mum's mobility needs but stood empty after my dad had a massive stroke and my mum by this time was suffering from chronic dementia (we were to lose her to this horrible condition in November 2015), I looked after the cottage and lived in the adapted holiday let whilst both my parents were in Gwyneth hospital Bangor. I was basically in self-imposed exile in the middle of nowhere as the property was half a mile from the next property. It was then that I started writing verses about my upbringing and past times. I was born in a pub in Liverpool and then stayed at my grandparents a lot in Huyton, Dovecot and Knotty Ash before moving over to the Wirral at 12 Slatey Road, Oxton at first before settling in Seacombe Wallasey as a five-year-old. I lost my biological mum in 1967 when I had just turned six and it was a few years before my dad remarried making a family of nine living in a two-and-a-box Merseyside terrace. Besides living and working abroad I travelled and stayed in many places from London to Glasgow and these 'anecdotes in rhyme' (I don't class myself as a poet, or these pieces as poetry) are a one size fits all for every working and middle-class towns and cities in the UK. I, of course, mention Merseyside in the synopsis introducing each piece. Particularly my beloved spiritual and childhood (from four-years-old) home of Seacombe. I stress though that these pieces are universal and are part of everyone in the UK's nostalgia banks (just change names and places) as to how we all lived mainly in past decades although there are some contemporary pieces. None of the expletives in very few (4 at most) of my pieces are gratuitous. They are written in my exact recollection of the language used in builders yards and public houses schoolyards etc. Asterix have been used in the more 'colourful' pieces. I hope to take the reader on a fantastic nostalgic ride. I never had any intention of publishing, I just used to post every morning on my FB group as a conversation starter to send a lifeline out to the millions of lonely people* and was absolutely overwhelmed by the thousands of requests to publish. It wasn't until I was shortlisted for the Roger McGough/Liverpool gin competition that I realised I had a gift to help people interact and hopefully I've brightened up many a depressed soul. Well here we go with part one of 'endearing (and not so endearing) observations.'

I hope it gives you all some wonderful recollections and topical observations.

Tony Usher

This piece although entitled *A Mersey Child* works in all the UK working class areas of the 50s through 70s, I hope it resonates with you all and brings back some fond memories.

Much love, T U.

A Mersey Child

A Mersey Child

All the back jiggers
Smelt of liver and onions
And most of yer grandmas
Had chilblains and bunions.

And most of the men
Drank brown bitter
Or mild
When I was a Mersey child.

Number 8 had a plate glass front door
And an Axminster carpet as well.

"We all know where that came from
She's got a fancy man that one
She never bought them herself, did she hell!"

And her nets are never white
Her mother was the same
Fur coat no knickers, and wild.

But when she passed them
They'd say
"You're looking fab Rosie May."

When I was a Mersey child.

"Get up yer own end"
Came the snobs daily rant

When you crossed that invisible line.

We'd shout.

"Piss off missus it's our road as well.
And ya stink of barley wine!"

Then she'd leg us
Down "our own end."

Pissed as a fart
Belching out obscenities
And bile.

A daily occurrence
In every one's street
If you were a Mersey child.

After church on Sunday
(For all you left footers)
Dad would have his couple of hours down the pub.

In his best Burton's suit

And new darts too boot

He was definitely on to a winner

And with a couple of bottles of stout for me Nan

He'd make his way home
To carve dinner!

On Friday for us lot
Fish only allowed

A bit of finny haddock
Or kippers

"What's that? You had cod
Ya stuffy little sod"

None of that for any of our nippers

But we were grateful for what we got

And when finished

We'd digest our food
And smile

And when we were able
Say "may I please leave the table?"

That's how it was

For a Mersey Child

We'd never dream of playing

Outside of the street
Without a big brother or two

And if went to the park
For high jinx and a lark

We were told
Watch yourself
In them loos!

Monkey bars
Witches hat
Swings and two slides

A typical playground
For a Mersey child

And as soon as we seen
The first streetlamp go on

We'd stop what we were doing

And break into a run

Back home
For some supper then bed

Where we'd kneel
And say evening prayers
To God

And in just a short while
This small Mersey child

Would be "fasto" (fast asleep)
In the great land of nod!

This is a piece about a man that lived on our road when I was a pre-teen kid overseeing everything and everyone. Most streets had a Jeremy / Jemima in the 60-70s who had a past life that us as kids couldn't envisage as all we had ever seen was a somewhat melancholy and his cat.

Jeremy

For those of you that never read the original draught this is simply titled *Jeremy*. Every street seemed to have a lost soul like Jeremy during my childhood, though their names, sex and back-stories differed slightly they were all of the same unmistakably gentle persuasion and carried a melancholy "air" with them. Hope it jogs your memories.

Jeremy was a mystery man
We knew his house and his name

But we never knew what he was about
His back-story? What's his game?

Most streets or areas
Had a Jeremy
Who all had a different title

And thinking back again
They could be a woman or a man
But to our hero
In this piece
That ain't so vital.

Macca had his Eleanor Rigby
And father McKenzie too
But it was Jeremy's ilk
That stood out from my past
He's a character that will relate to you.
As kids we would often
tiptoe past his house
Old brown paint behind privets overgrown

And watch him exit his casa
As quite as a mouse
To catch the number 33
 into town

Always dressed the same
Ankle length grey Mac' and flat cap
To explore what treasured bargains
Could be found.

None of us knew were Jeremy worked
Or if he ever socialised
He barely ever spoke or made a sound.

Just a nice timid man
Carrying on the best one can
Doing his best to avert our prying eyes

We knew he had a cat
As he'd feed it on his doorstep
Only the best
Al fresco dining for jeggsy's puss!

And when he seen us passing by
He'd wave at us painfully shy
Though looking back
I'm sure he was longing to talk to us.

Of the beautiful days
With his long passed wife
His reason for living- the spark in his life...

We'd heard it said
He'd been commissioned for bravery
During the war
But Jeremy's like never mentioned stuff like that

Living a mundane life
With only memories of his wife
An " oh so slow " day at a time
Just him and his cat

But I'm sure he came out to hear our laughter
Whilst feeding his feline friend outside his door

If only I'd have made the effort
To help him out a little bit more

Like pull his trolley to the bus stop
Or see him safely to his door.

We were told don't talk to strangers
But Jeremy was far from that
Just a shy ageing man
Nevertheless one of us.

And if he seemed a little odd
Who could blame the poor wretched sod?
We couldn't even help him off the bus!

None of us knew when Jeremy passed
No curtains drawn nor flags half mast

Life carried on without seeming to miss a step

The only clue to his sad demise
Was a poor old moggy with huge sad eyes
Who sat mournfully pining for him
On the step
were his food bowl once was kept.

Those of you old enough...help a Jeremy when you can even
if it's only giving him the time of day. For all I know Jeremy
from my street's action in WWII could be the reason I'm
alive and able to write. 90% of us in isolation definitely have
more human interaction than the Jeremys of my past had
and there are still Jeremys (and Jemimas a plenty) that you
can help. This sick world needs the individual human touch
and most of us possess it so please you all know the score.

I was born in Liverpool 7, spent times between the Vine pub (living above it in Vine Street) and the pubs in Huyton and grandmothers in Huyton and Notty Ash as before moving temporarily to the top floor of a huge Victorian mansion in Slatey Rd Oxton Birkenhead. I therefore have a love for most of Merseyside but particularly Seacombe just a mile from the world's famous waterfront that was the sight I would gaze upon whist playing as a teenager in Desmene St Park, Seacombe, this is a homage to the green / brown artery that both sides of the Mersey fed off and what a mother our magnificent Mersey is.

Much love, T U

Mersey Homage

Mersey Homage Part 1

Silhouetted 'gainst terraced sky's
A Mersey swallow
Soars and flies

And swooping way down low bellies
The frost on factory slate

Cuboid and gothic architecture
Mis-mashed on the palette of our river
Mythical birds perched high aloft twin towers

Set in new concrete replacing stone
They see each grimace, hear each groan
Gossamer sentinels eking away the hours

Life blood flowing way below
Metal boxes to and fro

From sun kissed islands and mighty logging streams

Tug boats ferry boats
River queens

Southerly ports
And refinery's lean

'Gainst opposite sides
Off a muddy green/ brown artery

The terraces bow to the Mersey's might

On shrill early morn's
And black winters night

Feel the power of ten million souls passed on!

Writers' mournful, poets cheeky

Artists ambitious
Smugglers sneaky

The music reaching the ears of the world

Buildings of Roman/ Greco style
Telling great untruths about their age

Market traders' millennia old
Shout out their wares
Clear loud and bold

Eateries from every quarter's palate
Octopus and finny haddock

Chinese, Caribbean,
Italian, tapas
And eastern Balti

A thousand years of sea faring men
Bring to our docks again and again

The spice, and of course the tried and tested "salty"

Our great city blends its skyline
All now clean and fresh and shiny

With the now sparse
"Dark satanic mills"
On the opposite banks of the Brinney

A heart divided
By a mighty tide

Feared and respected
By either side
A common people
Disected by a sweet smelling stench

This is a tale of a true story, you decide accordingly I experienced whilst walking home to Seacombe Ferry on a godless stormy night on the promenade from New Brighton – scary.

A Walk on the Prom

Making my way home one stormy wind swept night
As the wind cried Mary and the rain gave no respite
And a minute felt like an hour had passed
When through the fog my eyes espied the outline of a mast
'Twas reassuring to make out ye old black pearl
But atop her
'Gainst the safety rails was the figure of a girl
She was wailing and sobbing
Eyes full of woe and fright
That poor frightened woman all alone
As the tempest raged through the night
She pulled down her hood of scarlet red against the wind so chill
I couldn't see her properly as she turned and stood stock still
Pray tell me why you are out here mam
This is not a night to roam
Get in and batten down your hatches
Tonight's a night to stay at home
Then as she stood in hat and shawl I saw she held a lamp
She said it's to find my way to the ship wreck here
Through the driving rain and damp
I had to stifle a little laugh
She was two cannons short of a galleon poor girl
And I explained that ain't a shipwreck mam
It's just our ole faithful black pearl
So, I linked her as we battled through to the corner of Caithness Drive
To the place where she did abide
I said now hurry and get inside
While you're in one piece alive
She said don't worry lad you do not know me
If not you ain't no local lubber
And as she pulled down her red hoodie I heard
The cackle of the infamous mother.

This is for all people of a certain age that used to make the acquaintance of a young lady/ man whilst waiting for a taxi at the nearest rank to the nightclub from which you had just alighted. Many a phone number was scrawled on a page ripped out of the directory page in the phone booth next to the cab office and I know lads and girls that are still together only with kids and grandkids 40 years later after meeting on that beautifully alcohol-tinged night, I hope you're two of them.

Much love, T U.

80s Love

80's Love

You'd usually meet at the top of the street
At the taxi base up from the clubs
Your heads feeling light
As you'd been drinking sh**e
Extra strong earlier on at the pub

And to insignificance
Your confidence would pail

'Neath her 'heddy aroma
Of perfume and ale

And her kiss was like finding
Your own "holy grail"

This was courtin' 80s style!

The lad with the clipboard
Would take down your name

And you'd boast "we're together pal
Put us down as same!"

And whilst waiting
If she sat on your knee
She was game!

Wishful thinking 80s style!

Into the taxi and it's "drop her off first"
The age of chivalry still strong

And you were dying for a burst

And don't forget to get her house
Phone number first!

Priority's 80s style!

So you taxi'd her home
To the far end of town

For a peck on the cheek
With your window wound down

As you count your last coins
With a contemplative frown 😕

The cost of chivalry 80s style

So skint and back home
It's off up to bed

Where you dreamt
With her phone number
Next to your head

So glad you never tried
Her stuck up mate instead

Pickin' winners 80s style!

Any time between 5 and 7
It said
On the ripped out directory page
You'd took to your bed

And that's p.m. ya daft bugger
 Don't dare try A.M. instead!

Young loves impatience 80s style

And don't phone of a Sunday

The note also says

I know I'll bell her on Tuesday
Make her wait 2 full days

Treat 'em mean
Keep 'em keen
Isn't that what it says

Playing mind games 80s style

So teatime Tuesday eve
Your adrenalines at full throttle

But if her mam or dad answer
You'll well lose your bottle

Turn from man into mouse
Sat at "phone table"
In the house

Kackin' yer keks 80s style!

So the time eventually comes
When you get directly thru to "her"*

No mam or dad there just you two pair

And she tells you
She's with your "bessy" now
As she thought you didn't care!

Ya snooze ya loose 80s style!

It seems almost a hundred years ago that I got my first wage packet to make a hole in after a half chop (half day finish) in the local with the real men and women.

The banter from the locals was truly something to behold but today alas it has all but died.

Much love, T U.

The Banter Lies Dead

The day they turned a man into a mouse
was the day they shut down our public house
the local, the alehouse, pub or boozer
rich man, poor man, beggar or loser
it was your watering hole
after all you got to choose her!

But today the banter lies dead

Sat doing the crossword
Or just acting daft
Nursing your drinks
In bottles or on draught
Remember the days that we danced cried and laughed?

But today the banter lies dead

4 deep at the bar
We'd be waitin' for ages
To make a big hole in our first ever wages
"Get it down ya neck lad' it's only the early stages"

But today the banter lies dead

Shooting pool or playing cards
Arm wrestling and acting hard
"Don't be a prick kid, you'll only get barred"

But today the banter lies dead

Ale talk with the old guys who were nobody's fool
Flirting with the barmaids and being so cool
"They never taught me any of this at school"

But today the banter lies dead

Doubling up on your round
Getting ready for the band
And to curie their favour
You'd lend them a hand
To bring in all their gear from the back of their van (Gary
Murphy)

But today the banter lies dead

Quarter to midnight
Things getting a tad leery
Always posed for the boss
A nightly query
"Should I give 'em a lock-in, these f**ckers look scary"

But today the banter lies dead

Not many left now
All scattered far and near
In small towns like this
It's getting harder to drink a beer
With friends and great craic
I reckon this time next year

All! The banter will finally lie dead.!!

Looking back on the childhood of my youth to full employment a myriad of pubs, cafes and takeaways, today there are just a handful of pubs and an overabundance of eateries the detritus of the 80,000 houses, factories and commercial buildings would be spewed out by a pipe (or a few pipes). There was one at Seacombe ferry directly into our mile wide cesspit in which us young ones would gleefully swim every day when the current would allow us - how we never contracted typhoid or worse is beyond me.

This piece is mainly aimed at Seacombe, Poulton, Leasowe, Moreton with New Brighton to follow in part 2.

Much love, T U.

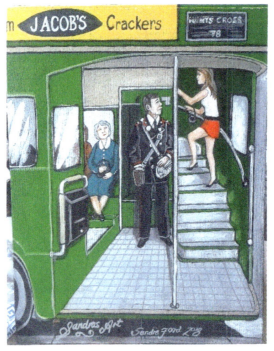

A trip around Wallasey

A Trip around Wallasey

A ferry without a pier
A town hall without a clock

A seaside with no deckchairs
But our very own "dome of the rock"

A brokey that's never been broken
And smugglers and wreckers that pillage

To a place with no tepees or a totem pole
That we know as the Indian village

The potteries the
The pipe cleaners

The washhouse
And kelvin motors

Were just a hop skip and jump
To where the council would pump

Seagulls welly's
Mersey burgers
And floaters!

Our very own Gandhy
With his very own belt

Our own smithy
And the wonderful
Metals he'd smelt

We had spillers and scotia
Our two favourite mills

Then up t' other end to Moreton
And squibs for your pills

They had a dangerous field
And its own pasture road

But no cows would graze there
Just ya' normal "frog and toad"

They've got an armchair with stools in
And had a plough that sold beer

But "The Farmers" was round the corner?
That always struck me as queer?

Their own "Willy Wonka's"
A factory of chocks

Were the workers could bring
Chocolate biscuits home

Only broken
In a brown bag or box

There's a brick works over in Tarran Way
Which you'd have to throw into the mix

If your little piggy was fussy
"Can't be doing with this straw or them sticks!"

Then backtracking through
To the Leasowe Estate

Of Wells Fargo and Dodge City fame
An oyster catcher that caught "feck all"
But sure knew how to play a good game

On the bill tonight folks
We ain't got the Beatles
Nor Cilla or Dana or Lulu

We've got "To drunk to funk
Getting drunk as some skunks
And a couple of hundred mad Zulu's!"

My tale don't stop here
Many pubs
Much more beer

And places where we all earned a crust

I'll probably be back tomorrow
With tales of mirth joy and sorrow

Destination?
Wally' village or bust!
Turning back onto Leasowe road
Past the solar powered school

And the Lidl that once had twenty rows

Onto the roundabout
Once so floral and gay

Were now barely anything grows.

The ship has now well and truly sailed
I watched its decline on my telly

The village now can boast merely
A handful of pubs

And that's including
Grove Road and "The Nelly"

But I must say the pub game
Ain't all doom and gloom

If I sound that way
I do beg your pardon

Coz the revamp they've done
On the old Cheshire cheese

Is spectacular
Check out its gin garden

Going back twenty years
Give or take

We were happy with porkies and yummies

But there's an over abundance of eateries now
More foodie gaffs than there are tummies

Five cafes
Three restaurants
That's not counting fast foods

Four chippies
Two pizza houses
Maybe three?

Then a subway
Four pie shops

And for that "genteel touch"

A tea room for scones
And high tea

Then further up the village
Just by my old school
I stop and take a glance over the road

And in my mind's eye
I'm taken right back

To the ashes
From which The Phoenix arose

Then there are the farmers and the lighthouse
Which I'm guessing are named

After locations and occupations

Were once the farmer had commanded
Come bye to his dog

And the lighthouse men signal
All hands to your stations

And yet more shops selling a myriad of things

Like carpets or flowers
A bridal gown
And party decorations!

(It all rhymes if read as I'm thinking it... you'll have to trust
me on that 'till I read it out on YouTube)

And of course there's the mandatory bookies
Or three!

'Spose a few of us like the odd flutter

But so many times people walk in there rich men

And come out crying
"That's me in the gutter"

So it's "WALLY WORLD"
The crème de la crème of our town

Were for most things
One pays nigh on double

It's no wonder
That under

Most folk's smiles
Lies a frown

As they sink under financial trouble

There's no cinema
No theatre

And no parking specks
You're hard pushed to find a genuine mate

Wallasey village??

I's fine for somet it my friend

Give me Seacombe
Or the Leasowe Estate! (Any day)!!

This piece delves into our first day at a new job especially as young apprentices and shows the ingenuity of the British working persons mischievous sense of humour.

Much love, T U.

Earning Your Stripes

A medium tin of "Elbow Grease" from down in the stores
A liberal splat of grease paint round your auld "town halls"
A can of tartan paint we were privy to them all

Back in our first day on the job

Getting sent to the Gaffa's office
By your new best mates
And told to ask the boss if you could have a long weight?
Your work mates putting the clock forward
So first day in you're "an hour late"
"I've never see the day through if I carry on at this rate."

The stick we took on our first day on the job

A nice glass hammer
Or a spirit level bubble
All things guaranteed a laugh
Your pals would go to any trouble
To have you feeling like a "burk"
On your very first day in work

How green we were that first day on the job

Taking tea into the heffer
Not knowing salt had been swapped for sugar
You knew damn well who the culprit was
But daren't rat out the bugger

You'd watch in horror as he took a sip
But work place "omerta"
Plus the threat of a thick lip
Would stop you blowing your mates up like a knob

But if you kept mum

And just stayed schtum
You'd be well in with the rest of um
When you turned up on your second day on the job.

Saturday Matinee

Saturday Matinee

Meandering our way to the A.B.C.
On windy wet Saturday morns
With our duffel coats and balaclavas on
Stopping to only to stock ourselves up
With Spanish gold and sherbet dabs
From Vaughan's

Then back on the track
With the wind at our backs
Kicking up leaves in the fall
We'd break into a run
Toward that palace of fun
To sing along with the bouncing ball

"Six tickets to the circle please
And a hand full of football chews"
And a fab or a zoom
To devour at the show
Whilst being watched
By the "monitor crews" (glorified brown- nose's)

Anyone's birthday today?
Asked the man
our "uncle"
up there on the stage
then some jammy sod
Would give him the nod
And climb up there
With proof of their age

To a big bag of goodies-and popcorn!
Or free tickets to next week's show
they'd increase in height
'Neath the cinema stage lights
a boost from the celebrity glow!

Watching 'loony tunes'
Clutching ABC Balloons
How we'd laugh
Crying tears of delight
But we knew before the 3 stooges came on
We'd be privy to "b movie" sh**e!

But after the stooges
or maybe Flash Gordon
or Lassie versus Rin Tin Tin
we'd wait with breath held
for the "film of the week"
to rejoice with an ear splitng din!

As the hero fought with the villain
We'd be shouting for more and more
Then we'd stamp with both feet at the villain's retreat
"Till we near enough crashed through the floor

And when the curtain came down
And the lights went on
The stage would look like a tip
With lolly ice wrappers
And Kia-ora cartons
Testimony of our cinema trip!

Do you remember the old Victorian / Georgian and even Edwardian libraries of yesteryear? This is how I recall the experience of these cathedrals of literature especially on inclement weather days.

From the unique comforting spell of parchment and must to the sound of silence and the joys of delving into Childhood classics, if any of you haven't watched the semi illuminated movie *The Page Master* you could do a lot worse, it's part of the inspiration for this piece.

Much love, T U.

Libraries of My Youth

Libraries sparsely lit in mid winter
The unique aroma of parchment and must

Not forgetting wood and metal polish
And the sound of silence... Shush!

Lead light windowpanes trembled
When the librarian stamped each book

Measuring 8.5 on the Richter scale
As bookshelves shuddered and shook!

That enveloping warm cocoon
That we all knew as "The Reading Room"
In which you'd shelter in the elements for hours

Sash weight windows let in an icy breeze
And when you couldn't stifle a sneeze
You'd be faced with forefingers on lips
And angry glowers!

But once said windows were closed tight
Against winter elements haughty might

The only sound that you would hear
Were the clanging of hot water and air

Running though the radiators
Lighting up your cheeks warm and bright

Torrential rain keeping you from home
As you engrossed yourself in your latest tome!

Balaclava and gloves laid on the table
A million miles away from Black Beauty's stable

As you let your imagination freely roam

Your fertile mind battling highwaymen
Or the one legged pirate "Long John again
Wind picking up with leaves whooshing by
As you snuggly settle in warm and dry

When you hear that rumbling thunder drawing near
And after glancing up
For a cursory look
Its head back down
And back to your book

All toasty and warm
Without the slightest hint of fear

It'll soon be time to make your way back home
So you wrap up well 'gainst the approaching storm

Balaclava and gloves and duffle coat back on
And head out into the tempest and all its fury

You make it safely to your doorstep
Books and all
Into your living room
Through vestibule and hall
To a cosy fireside
Where you resume your current story

The stamp on your ticket
Allows a quarter of a year
To indulge your fertile mind
With tales or daring, do and fear

Alas the library experience today
Doesn't even come near

To my wide eyed, toasty library days
Of yesteryear

Ho ho ho with the great gift of poetic licences I've been able to mix my situation of Christmas Day of times present with the fond memories I had on a Christmas Day as a child, teenager, and finally a young man, I think it works splendidly.

Much love, T U.

A Grandad's Christmas

A Grandad's Christmas

Wake with my head full of Christmas thoughts
to be greeted by Jason and his Argonauts
Watches that after having my scrub
Then off for a pint in the rub-a-dub-dub.

All me mates in their new bib and tucker
"I've got a 22lb turkey! Took me all night to pluck her" 😄

That's getting sizzled
Whilst I'm slightly sozzled
Can't stay out for hours like I once could
I've got to get home
Now I'm living alone
Check the turkey whilst basting the spuds.

Mmmm... That was nice
I could of ate it all twice
But gotta leave room for my pud
which is laced with brandy
Ooh that comes in handy
And why not?
It's Christmas
Life's good

A bit of trifle with jelly
Del boys on tele
Poor rodders always gets it in the ear
Then whilst scratching me knackers
Between cheese port and crackers
Just room to crack open a beer.

Then after opening no end of pants socks and smellies
It's under the stairs to root out me old welly's
Coz as I've been eating
Snows fallen down

And to walk of my fayre
I'm going to dare
To walk to the far side of town (and back)

So it's back to my T.V.
Can't miss the Bond movie
I'll admit I never watch to the end
I usually wake myself snoring
It's not that its boring
It's just that I'm exhausted my friend

I've never needed a reason
To show love at this season
Of festivity kindness and cheer
So get this while its going
Even if it ain't snowing
MERRY CHRISTMAS AND A HAPPY NEW YEAR!

I penned this at the start of the first lockdown trying to get across the stoicism and versatility of my beloved Merseyside and in particular an elderly couple that seem to have been around forever and are still in tip top shape.

Much love, T U.

Liverpool Lockdown

They've been a couple now for years
These two old folk I know
But still they look as young as the day they met

They've seen it all before
All the famine, plagues and war
But it ain't budged them
From their home as yet

You see they're well set in their ways
And they look back on glorious days
From their house they watched
The buildings of both tunnels

And they'd name every ship one can
From the ferries to Ireland and the Isle of Man
Plusall the passenger ships from White Star and Blue
Funnel

They'd always had a cracking view
When the boys in red
Or the lads in blue
Made their way towards Mann Island
In an open top bus

Where kids were tryna get a speck
Climbing up lampposts
Risking breaking their neck
They'd join in but never make a fuss

They'd just stand there back-to-back not saying much
Just enjoying the craic
And always got a better view
Than all of us

They were the grandest couple in all of town
On film stars and royalty theyd look down
But they weren't being pompous
In fact, I've never heard them say a word

And don't think I will till the day that I die
As they stand proud
300ft up in the sky
'Cause you see each one of this couple is a Liver Bird

Cast your minds back, if you will, to these long hot days as a child; I can smell the tar bubbles as we burst them.

Much love, T U.

Ally-oh

Ally-Oh

Filling old pop bottles with corporation pop and pretending
its white lemonade
Dressing up as fire bobbiess and never getting paid
Searching for hours for ammo
For an inter street nacker raid
And singing ally-oh all through the day

Playing in sh*t high bombdeys were we all forbidden to go
You'll catch impetigo then you'll soon bloody know
Being told that where you'd cut yaself
A pig's foot would miraculously grow

Singing ally-oh all through the day

Jumping on the back of wagons and riding them as long as you
can
The alpine lorry the skip wagon and the long gone bakers van
Copping for an unfortunate one if you were collared by the
man

And singing ally-oh all through the day

Pooling in your slummy for a nice hot 6 of chips
Cramming them in our gobs so fast we'd blister all our lips
Not worrying back then about them putting pounds on your
hips

Still singing ally-oh all through the day

Legging it home through the backway but before traipsing
in through the kitchen door
Leaving muddy shoes in the outside lav, we all knew the score
And hearing mam barking out her impossible demand
"Don't you dare walk on my floor"

And singing ally-oh all the way to bed.

This piece is all about stand out moments in my life, as the 60s morphed into the age of Aquarius the brand-new super optimism 70s. I hope it jogs a lot of fond memories.

Much love, T U.

Back Flashes of my Young Life

Being transfixed
By the sight of a hippy

Buying my first "six of chips"
From the chippy

Getting a clip around my ear
For being lippy
Oh the joy of my 60s years

Waiting all year
For the fair
To hit the park

Knocking on doors
Then hiding
For a lark

The bogey man will get you
If you stay out after dark!

Worked every time for this 60's child

Spending hours in the park
Jumping moats and climbing trees

In the words of Terry Jacks
We skimmed our hearts
And skimmed our knees

Then the Isley brothers came
With their sweet Summer Breeze
As I morphed into a 70's child

Dreaming of me owning
A brand-new Raleigh Chopper

Running recklessly over Liscard Road
And nearly coming a cropper

Yer mam making ya swallow
Cod liver oil
Was you really going to stop her?

"It'll grow hairs on yer chest
You pasty faced 70's child!"
(Even the girls down our street)

Platform shoes
And bright coloured flares

Three and five star jumpers
And feather cut hair
Bunking on the bus
Or in the cinema
Who cares?

Not me!
I'm now a 70's child!

Ape hangers
Banana seats
Cards on the spokes of your wheels
Hand sprayed down your back jigger
Nearly as good
As the real deal

And to get it on the road
We would beg, borrow and steal

All part of the fun for this 70's child!

My memories of getting abruptly woken up after being shouted at numerous times. To the bus trip, the school yard and eventually assembly, we would often recall last night's movie or play for the day that was on after the watershed or was deemed too X-rated by our parents to view. So us mere school kids that didn't get the chance or permission to watch would join in the debate of said show and just jump in every now and again, "yeh, remember this part" and relay something already relayed by one of our fellow pupils - all pure bluff.

Much love, T U.

Off to School

Off to School

Get up
rise and shine
Shake a leg
Get out your bed
Wet flannel under arms and face
Then drag a comb through your tatty head
Its half past eight
You're always bloomin' late
Get ya breaky
Hurry, rush
Then I leg it up stairs
Trippin' over me flares
To give me toofys a brush
Still running late
Me mates at the gate
Leg it lar
Or we'll miss the bus
I say relax you fool
Well only be late for school
Cool yer boots
And stop making a fuss
So we just make the bus
By the skin of our teeth
And roughly push our way up the stairs
Yesss! No inspector!
Well that's a relief
This morn we won't be paying any fares
Alas just two stops later
The man from Jamaica
Decides hell take our bus today
Its inspector "Big Vic"
Who doesn't miss a trick
Looks like we'll just have to pay
Throwing paper and chewy
And things sticky and gooey

At the other school
Backed up down the stairs
Boys slagging the girls
About their ringlets and curls
Knowing deep down
You fancied them
But who cares?
The main talking point
Was last night's TV
On which one would articulate
Bluffing your way through
About the movie
They viewed
Although for you
It was on far too late
But one had to be seen
To be well in the know
About last nights
Televisual show
Yesss you'd bluffed your way through
Jeez that was close ''Phew''
Then you'd alright your bus trip
With a hop and a skip
To be welcomed as ''one of the few''
That went to bed after ten
Next day you'd bluff through again
It wasn't hard just copy your peers
Throwing in
Every now and again
The appropriate laughs groans and jeers
Then onto the school ground
Before the bell rang
To make your way to assembly
Then classes
All seems like yesterday
So get out
And make hay

Because it's frightening
How quick our time passes
From fooling at school
To your years
Of acting cool
You know times flies by
With each passing yule
So cram into your lifetimes
All the good things you can
At a steady pace
Don't make a great fuss
Live life
With one gleeful shout
Make sure you know what it's all about
Before it's our stop
To alight the bus

The bittersweet years of one's first day at school/nursery, the freedom of being allowed to play in the local park by yourself, your first true lovers kiss and of course your first pint.

Much love, T U.

Dent in it (Angst and the Heart)

When you start thinking back on the things you miss
All the 18ths, 21st's and Christmases
And the things you miss are oh so many
You have to make a list

Your heart will get a dent in it

From that very first day in school
When we never stood a chance
When your mum has left and you were sat
Trying not to spoil your pants
And you sweep back all them years
To see your mama's parting glance

Your heart will grow a dent in it

Them halcyon days
Of swings, lakes and parks
The thrill of playing hooky
Or playing out after dark
Your first summer holidays
Full of scrapes, japes and larks

Your heart will grow a dent in it

Your first years in middle school
When things began to change
And true loves kiss
Was drawing ever nearer into range
When just one look at your school yard crush
Made your tummy feel all strange

Your heart will grow a dent in it

Your very first time of getting served
Giving it large down the local
Although you stood out like a farmer's boy
Or some kind of alien yokel

And you'd get well pis *ed
On a pint of Scotch Mist
And get launched out
For being mega local

Your heart will grow a dent in it

When you're alone at night
With thoughts of yesteryear's delights
When everything seemed rose tinted
And magical and bright
Don't emit the thoughts
That make your heart shine not as bright

Or your heart will grow a dent in it!

This recalls our first day of a new term and for a lot of us, a new year or holiest of holies, a brand-new school. We were turned out brand spanking new or as good as, we were all immaculate or immaculate stage 2 and God forbid if we scuffed or tore our new school outfits before the allotted number of days set out by our parents.

Much love, T U.

Back to School

Back to School

Approving looks from Grandma and Grandad
Hair combed back like "our Lords can lad"
In a new barrafier
That's uber cool
And "stay pressed" kecks
For your first day back at school

The girls were the same
Only they wore skirts
Lads were posers
Girls were flirts
Practical or provident
Whichever yer ma would choose
Then down to get your uniform
From T.J. Hughes

Not forgetting something new for your feet
Can't go traipsing round
In ya bare plates of meat
And best place to beat
Them new school blues?
Freeman, Hardy & Willis
For your Solicitors shoes

If you were only changing year
No new rig out for you
But your ma would try her best
To have you looking brand new

With a new button here
and a stitch in time there
And the tightest of finetooth combs
Dragged through your hair
Which you'd had Voseene'd twice
The evening before!

To coffier a shiny new barnett
For that little bit more

Bit of glue or Velcro
To let down turn ups and hems
Creased out with an iron steaming hot
Blakeys and segs
For last year's shoes
Made to shine with Cherry Blossom
And off ya trott

New satchels or bags
If you were quite well off
Complete with new geometry set
Made one quite the bleeding toff
But once you hit that playground
Make sure no one had you off

(Stealing new pupils gear was rife… geometry sets, school
bags etc... in tolerated)
The ups and downs of your first new term in school!

Those once-a-week family nights that unfortunately are all too easy to come by today, a case of less is more definitely.

Much love, T U.

Staying Up Late

Round to the sweet shop with dad's order for sweets

To whack out
Between us
A most welcome rare treat

Oh, and that was just the beginning
Oh yes that was great

But just the precursor
To staying up late!

Squeezed tight on the couch
Or spread out by the fire

Sucking on fruit drops
To our little hearts desire

Lights go off
And the film comes on

"Swap you 3 liquorish all sorts
For a toffee bon bon?"

Each of us guarding
Our sweets laden plate

Highlight of the week
We're staying up late

Norman Wisdom
George Formby
Or maybe Will Hay

Or a nice Ealing comedy
Would make anyone's day!

That special family evening
When we'd all make a date

To gather around the telly
And stay up till late!

Each of us trying
To make "our" sweets last longer

So you could bring out your toffees and gloat

I see you've finished all yours

Well I hope you don't mind

Me scoffing these I hid in me coat

Then the pitter patter
Of rain on the window
And the wind picking well up outside

Us all bathed in that lovely warm glow from the tele
Just the night to be lounging inside

And as you hear people running
To get in from the rain

And get their tootsies
Warmed up by the grate

You put on the air
Of a mill I on aire

Ooooh the luxury
Of staying up late

Elvis or Cliff were great family favs
Or William Tell or Rob Roy
With their entourage of "braves"

And when the evening was over
We traipse up to our beds

With songs of "the king"
Spinning round in our heads

Nowadays kids have Netflix and movie channels galore

Too much taken for granted of late

But we hit our joyful peak

If we're lucky
Once a week

When the family
All stayed up late!

What it says on the tin, a contemporary tale of a very special child swapping Bethlehem for Aintree.

Much love, T U.

A Scouse Nativity

A Scouse Nativity

Me and my two brothers
One cold December day
Decided to go for a jar

We all had a few bob
So we went up the shops
Before gleefully hitting our first bar

Each of us
All sons of old Mrs King
Who lived in the east of the city

All three of us, each with our own different quirk
One rich, one flash and one pretty

Into Boodle & Dunthorn
The three of us traipsed
Our kid liked a nice piece of gold...
Jewellery to wear (it went with his hair)
Then back out to the snow and the cold

Next into John Lewis
To the aftershave counters
For the second of Mrs King's boys

Some Aramis 900
To slap on his chops
Before hitting town making noise

While in John Lewis
I decided to nip
To house hold goods on the next floor

For potpourri or scent
Of a cinnamon bent
To place by my vestibule door

Mmm cinnamon and wine
That scent seemed just fine
"We're done here"
And we vacate the shop floor

So off on our pub crawl
We three brothers King
Stepped into our first port of call

We were greeted with some news
Which gave us the blues
Off a big baldy barman, named Paul
"You know Mary & Joe
That live by   Ma's"

Asked Paul rhetorically
Whilst pulling a mild
"Well the hossys on shutdown
And the hotels are chocka

And poor Joey's wife
Is with child!"

By this time
Eventide had fell all around

All the three of us each nursed a jar

"Don't just stand there"
Yelled Paul

And continued to bawl

'Get out there and follow that star"

So the three of us

Jumped in the back of a hack
"Where to?"
Asked the amicable driver

"Just follow that star"
It don't look too far
It won't be much more than a fiver

"Don't worry about dollar"
Said the taxi driver fella
"It's cool I know the gaff well"

And with a twinkle in his eyes
To the three king's surprise
He said
"My name is Gabriel"

"Have you come from afar?"
Asked the driver of the car
"And did you all come bearing gifts?"

To which they replied,
"We're all from the east side"
And nice one Gabby for the free lift

They said, "we bought this stuff here
Before going for a beer"
Showing the celestial driver
Their purchases

And with his foot on the gas
Using his rear-view glass
Exclaimed
"Thanks lads, you're truly three aces"

So through the traffic they raced
At a shooting stars pace
Until they reached the old stables
By Aintree

And in the hush of the night
Beheld the glorious sight
Just lying there
In a crib down the entry

So down the dirt track
Ventured the three brothers

To the glow
Shining out from the stable

And to their wondrous eyes
Full of awe and surprise

Was a manger with child
On the table

In old Aintree
Down Bethleham Road
Lay the child

Master of heaven and hell

And all dressed in yuletide Bessy's
They brought forth their pressy's

To the Christ child
Emmanuelle!

Well I hope you all liked my contemporary tale
Of the birth
A tale most of you know well

Me? I'm off on the wing
With the three brothers' king

If we're lucky we'll catch the last bell

A look back at the age-old traditions and occurrences that make for a nostalgic feast, the type I find irresistible.

Much love, T U.

As Time Hurtles On

Talking to your neighbours over the back yard wall

Putting out your bottles when the twilight falls

It never even entered our heads

That we would miss these things at all

All lost as time hurtles on

Hiding in your house when the tally man called

Milk, gas and leccy we were in hock with them all

The grind of paying them off, your debts at a snail's pace crawl

Still here as time hurtles on

Rising every morn at 6 to heat one room

With coke or coal

Scuttled in on cold wet winter morns

It could nigh or break your soul

7 of us eating watery porridge from just two bowls

Hard to imagine now as time hurtles on

Side cars for motorbikes in almost every street

Using starting handles to start your car

Come snow, hail, rain or sleet

Or throwing eggs in your radiator to seal it tight and neat

Things all lost to us (for the better)

As time hurtles on

Sneaking into the front room

That was saved for best and guest

To quietly dance to the radiogram

In yer undies and yer vest

And heaven forbid if you broke anything

You'd spend the bleeding rest

Of the week indoors

As time crept slowly on

Putting creases in your ironing

Using old brown paper bags

Using a bookies runner

For your flutter on the nags

For which you'd listen on the wireless

Whilst making your way through a hundred flags

All up in smoke

As time hurtles on

Working at the news agents

Delivering for the man

Or maybe graft for the local grocer

Dropping off goodies for the kitchen pans

But delivery boys are few and far between

As things now stand

Soon to be gone, as time hurtles on

Young mums in their bras

Chatting in your street on sweltering hot summer days

Retrieving your casey from old grumpy's back yard

In all sorts of ingenious ways

Finding a thousand things to do

In them hot long summer days

Life was slower

Before time started hurtling on, the times we had playing games and making our own entertainment from dawn till dusk in them oh so safe days of our yesterdays are such happy times.

Much love, T U.

Childhood Games

Childhood Games

Queenie – I, off ground tick, shammy 1,2-3
Come play some old-fashioned games with me
Jumping off walls
Best man falls
Football, Rugby, Cricket, Tennis – simple things – just balls
(ooh missus!!)

From Breakfast to tea-time
Packed sarnies in between
We were all a small part
Of one big winning team

Forget the score
The end result
If we played bad or good
We'd limp home smiling from ear to ear
Through the gob full of municipal mud

Hopscotch
Two – Balls
Split the bleeding kipper (ouch)
Cost next to nowt for fun and japes
When I was a scruffy wee nipper

Running through the rose gardens (naughty)
Climbing high walls (allowed?)
Jumping moats and climbing trees
When we couldn't find our balls.

Can we have our ball back 'Pleeeease, Mister'
Put that knife away
Well chip in for your new kitchen window
We only came to play
(shouldn't have kitchen windows behind our goalmouth
anyway!)

Shuv ha'penny, all our men
Picking winning teams
The local park was Wembley
Or the stadium of our dreams

Murder ball
Skipping rope
Swimming in the river
Living proof you don't need
Mega-gigabytes to deliver

The enormous fun from dawn till dusk
To sate our playful souls
Delivered by a spade and a sandy beach
That we'd spatter with assorted holes!

Chases off the parky
Often with their dogs
Risky if one of the dodgier ones found you
After dark in the public bogs

(hands on your ha'pennies)

That was a lifetime ago
We would rarely feel low
And gay meant a different thing
Just a gang of us and a bag full of lollies
Oh how my heart would sing

The comradeship that bonding gel
That camaraderie
The games belonged to all of us
 not "1 for you and 2 for me"

and even though we'd often
splinter off in different gangs
we'd still be one big happy crew
barra bing barra boom barra bang

(You don't see that anymore)

I could have written a book on this note sized piece of our yesterdays, close your eyes after reading and soak in the wonderful world of yesterday, now all but disappeared for the better. You tell me.

Much love, T U.

A Huge Leap Forward (Ya Don't See That Anymore)

Throwing buckets of water over amorous dogs

Reading rude graffiti scrawled in public bogs

Back row of the flicks for a smooch and a snog

Ya don't see that anymore

Entering your house through a mucky back entry

Gentlemen of the road

Talking like lorded gentry

Schools with wonderful names

Like St. Aloysius Elementary

Ya don't see that any more

Dads with their kecks rolled up

Paddling in the Mersey

Hankies knotted on their heads

Still in shirt sleeves and jersey

And as for us in our tatty grotts

Well lord have mercy

Ya don't see that anymore

Out in all kinds of weather

To go the outdoor loo

Legging it downstairs in one sock and shoe

We couldn't very well use the po

To have a number two

Ya don't see that anymore

Kids racing karts

Down the local hill

Workers in pet shops

Caught with their fingers
in the trill

Needing a letter off the pope

For the contraceptive pill

Ya don't see that anymore

Overladen ferries

With people going to work

When folk never knew the meaning

Of words like skive or shirk

Names like ya divvy

Or ya stupid burke

Ya don't see (or hear) that anymore

Getting knocked back from night clubs

For not wearing a tie

Not tapping off because you were painfully shy

Getting collared by the ten to two birds

(only girls left without a partner when the slowy's were winding down)

Good god I'd rather die

Phew, ya don't see that anymore

Got to say goodbye now

But it wouldn't be right

For me to finish off

And say goodnight

Without a great big 60's mention

Of the white dog sh**e

Because

Ya don't see that anymore

This is recalling my years in and around the Church Street area of Egremont, not to be confused with Church Rd half a mile down the road (see *The Pit and The Square*), particularly with the Little family and Harpo Little, a huge character in the Church Street area.

Much love, T U.

Church Street

Church Street Days

Sitting on garage roof full of big ideas
Scrapping in the gutter, cauliflower ears?
No you can't eat them, they're not for your tea!

It's a personal thing, just you and me!

And half of Church Street and Union Street too
Feck it throw in Darlington Street they can all come and view.

5 in a phone box it's freezing outside

Let's all go down Maddocks slip
Play chicken with the tide

Then over to the red-grah for a game of footy

Its 10 o'clock its pissin' down
Never said we wasn't nutty

Me mate lives in 104
He's got a boss shed

He swears Bob Marley lives there
Even after he was dead

I often stay in Harpo's
I know his mum and dad

They take in all the waif's and stray's
So nice, but must be mad

Tool up quick boys
I know that distant humming

Its them scooter boys from Birkenhead
Come cruising for a drumming

It's cleared up today
Let's pool in all our dosh

A case of Merrydown from Checklands
Let's all get f***ing sloshed

Then over for a game of pool
Jack won't mind

As long as his tills are ringin'
Everything gonna be just fine

Then later on well climb on top
Of some poor workies van

Watch exotic dancer through The Shepherds window
Can't wait to be a man

Over to The Acropolis
We're starvin' but no cash

Chicken and chips twice please boss
100 yard dash
It's throwin' out time soon
We may just spy a fight

Or share a spliff under the Maissy's stairwell
If we can find one with a working light

I could go on and on and on
Wax lyrical in so many ways

We didn't have much money
But got more than our taste of honey

In my Halcyon Church Street days

To peruse whilst sitting comfortably on the BEST seat in the house.

Much love, T U.

Tales From the Little Room

When I was young and into my tunes
My grandma was keen on roughage and prunes

Now as I grow older
I do the best that I can
To eat a lot less eggs
Spend less time on the pan

I pray to the lord
Eyes raised to the sky
To drop everything quick
Be a regular guy!

Yes as I grow older
And things start to get blocked
I eat a shedload of fibre
To keep the tummy unlocked

The more meds I'm prescribed
It seems I have waited
Half of a lifetime
To stop being constipated!

If this ditty's offensive
An assault on your ear
You can skip to the next one
All about diarrhoea

So for all of you
That just don't like it one bit
I trot off to the loo
For my regular s**t

Coz I've now joined the gang
Of old fogies and loons
Who wake every morning
To roughage and prunes

A piece all about making pub/club crawl from Seacombe to New Brighton, and later on in life Liscard tramps/Christies.

I make no excuse for the colourful Anglo-Saxon expletives as they are in keeping with the narrative and never gratuitous.

Much love, T U.

Night Out Anyone?

Night Out Anyone?

The Nelly, The Welly, The Boot, The Bars and The Dale
Falcon hair-sprayed and denimed up
For a night on the town on the ale!

Starting off slow with a pint of lager
Or maybe a little pale ale (Toby Light – just right)
Then onto snakebites and Pernod and black chasers
With the wind firmly at our sails!

I mean what's the use in getting dressed up
To stay out on 2% ale
After all when we'd had a couple off the top shelf
We were men of iron... not frail

With our shoulders pushed back
And our Johnny concrete swagger
(we're the elite, we don't accept laggers)

We're off to be kings of the ale
Taking up both sides of Borough Road
Heading for the bright lights of Dale!

And when we had "Coke"
It was in vodka
With a smoke
Of sovereign, number 6 or number 10

And we'd smoke playing pool
Or at the bar or at our stool
No "please smoke outside" rules back then

Then Liscard or New Brighton
For women and fighting
As many as ya liked in a cab

We'd keep the driver waiting
Whilst silently hating
While we stopped for a donner kebab

Spilling beer, food and more
Over his seats and floor
As he glanced in his rear-view glass

Did he fancy the odds
Against these horrible sods
And take the chance of being put on his ass!

But he'd usually hedge his bets
Knowing after a couple more wets
They'll all end up sprawled out on the grass!

Coz with their veins full of fightin'
They'd get dropped in New Brighton
At The Grand or Guinea or Penny clubs
All named after money
Which when looking back is funny
Coz when we got there we never had any!

So it's in through the back way
Unless you knew the doorman
Who'd you think "go on kid it not my money"
F**k it

But if when you got in
You were collared minesweeping
You'd be better off kicking the bucket!

You'd get launched down them stairs
With a who f*ckin cares?
It's my job you put on the line!

Just straighten yer tie
You ain't gonna die
Try next door
They're all daft
You'll be fine!

So after trying the others
And having no luck
It's that lonely walk home down the prom

And if you're lucky you'd find some pissed
High-heeled girl stragglers
Who'd just met the same fate as you

And if your face didn't fit
Then who gave a sh*t
I'll try again next week
Toodle-oo

I hear a lot of people moaning far too much about social distancing and lockdown when in reality we are a small percentage of our planet that are so spoiled compared with the other poor wretched souls that we inhabit this planet with. It is also us that are pushing the ecology towards the precipice of no return. Start lending a hand.

You've Never Had it So Good

YOU'VE NEVER HAD IT SO GOOD

Watching a good programme on this evenings telly
Clean clothes and bedding
When things start getting smelly
And never having to worry about an empty belly

YOU'VE NEVER HAD IT SO GOOD

Looking out your window at a sycamore ridge
A solo walk around the park
Skimming stones or crossing a bridge
And then it may just be a nice cold beer or fruit juice out
the fridge

YOU'VE NEVER HAD IT SO GOOD

Flicking on a switch and "hey presto let there be light"
To help you from your bedroom
In the dead of night
To a flushing bog a luxury
That takes away ones s**te!

YOU'VE NEVER HAD IT SO GOOD

The daily pampering of yourself
In the shower or the bath
Even if its avocado green
There's f**ck all wrong with naff!
Or simply reading my little ditties
And hopefully getting a laugh

YOU'VE NEVER HAD IT SO GOOD

Getting daily exercise
By pounding empty streets
Coming back to a nice hot Ralgex footbath for your feet
To billions these things are
An extraordinary treat

YOU'VE NEVER HAD IT SO GOOD

Daily interactive contact
Digitally connected through time and space
Whatsapping your kin
In the blink of an eye
In Australia or the States
You not only get to chat with them
You can see their smiling face

YOU'VE NEVER HAD IT SO GOOD

These are pure luxuries
Gifted to the few
By a benevolent "God of good"

That chose us ungrateful thankless lot
Its always puzzled me why he should

Choose us above all others
Me? I'd change it if I could

And give these bounties
To the wretched poor who drink and wash in rivers of mud

BECAUSE THEY REALLY HAVEN'T HAD
ANYTHING SO GOOD.😖

The perils of a 60s & 70s newspaper delivery boy. Again the language is in keeping with my feelings to being used as slave labour by a very angry grumpy newsagent for years.

Early Morns

Early Morns

Please keep the noise down

Husband on nights

Sellotaped to the window

In plain black and white

They'd all got home an hour before me

As it was just getting light

When I was a newsagent's boy

Stumbling around the bedroom

Trying not to wake me brothers

Huddled together using old coats for covers

Then tiptoe past mam and dad's room

I daren't wake the lovers

When I was a newsagent's boy

Then quietly down the stairs

Navigating each creak

And out through the backway

Before day did break

Coat and hood pulled tight

Against the elements might

Oh the joys being a newsagent's boy

Battered shoes on cobbles

Battling black ice terrain

One step forward two steps back

Through the driving wind and rain

And every day I'd vow

I'd never do this again

A wind lashed rain sodden newsagent's boy

At last into the shop

Out of the tempest so dire

To try and dry out

Hogging the two bar leccy fire

Frostbitten fingers

And little blocks of ice had replaced all me toes

And a 3 inch icicle hanging down from me nose

Frosty the newsagent's boy

The shift workers all crowding in to buy fags

Coughing up phlegm like a bunch of old lags

With their 80 senior service gov

Or an ounce of rough shag

A bawdy giggle from the newsagent's boy

Then out into the maelstrom to deliver my wares

To post all neat and proper

Without the hint of a tear

Because if people complained

I'd have to beware

Of the wrath of the newspaper man

Battling on for hours

Down roads, copes and streets

Boulevards and avenues

What a glorious fecking treat

When I finish I'm gonna rob the fooker blind of all his sweets

That slave driving monster of a man

When I got home I'd have to get ready for school

Hardly time for any brekky

I must have been such a fool

But with the great gift of hindsight
Looking back

Its turned out quite cool

Coz I'm one mother f*****g tough old man and no one's
fool!

The Five Bars was my first ever local and along with the Shepard's, the Oyster Catcher and the Lord Nelson, a huge part of my life. In this piece I tell of the characters and camaraderie through my yearning to have my photo put on the rouges gallery full of me and women, all my heroes in their heyday. The closest I got was a photo of myself and my best mate Johnaboy Ralph and Seacombe Elnar Humphrey Kilby, not forgetting a fresh face 17-year-old Pete Molly Mitchell on Johnaboys 18th in December 1978.

Five Bars Wall

The Five Bars' Wall

I moved over to Seacombe when I was 2 foot tall
John, Gerrard, Tony, Jacqueline, Terry and Paul (Mick
came later)
In all that time my ambition was
Not to go to the Lord Mayor's ball
But to get me photo hung up
On the Five Bars' wall!!

Bobby Bennett, Tommy Jones
Three prices for the price of one
Reggie, Dave and Podger
(that was George to his dad and mum)
From Luke to Ralph Sullivan
They ranged from very tall to small
But the buggers had all their photos
On the Five Bars' wall!!

Another price behind the bar
Who married Geordie Dave
And the North East lad who'd seen it all
And taught me to behave
Another fine man
I will never understand
That the Lord didn't save
One of many
Off the Five Bars' wall

There were two great Anns
Behind our bar
Ann Rutter and Ann Wise
Then later Dave and Val
(who once was married to my pal)
Seacombe souls in a different guise
They all had one thing in common
And I was jealous of them all

Cause they all had their mugshots
On the Five Bars' wall

There were all the big families
Rutters, Ralphs, Cleareys and Kilbys
Some of them wore caps
And some hid slap heads
Beneath their trilbies
Watch nobody knocks your hat off
Pride always comes before a fall
And now instead of a tifter
There's a big baldy bonce
On the Five Bars' wall!!

What a motley crew they made
Jocks and Geordies
Paddys and Yids
And auld grumpy Jackie Beattie
Always shouting at us kids
We knew he loved us really
It was just one of the things he did
Whilst pursuing the pics
On the Five Bars' wall

Bobby in his corner
Crossword and pencil in hand
Ya know for all the years I drank in there
I only ever seen him stand
He'd race through the Guardian cryptic
Never asking for a hand
A genius behemoth
Straight off the five bars wall!

When I first started frequenting
"The Bars"
It was run by Bob and Joan
And sometimes when Bob was locking up

He'd say "fancy a Toby Tone?"
They had a house in Serpentine Road
And I'd walk him most the way home
It took no time at all
From the Five Bars' wall

My minds alive
With music and jive
Recalling my beautiful past
Just you and me
And the photo gallery
Some of them long since passed
And once a year
We should raise a beer
And fly and "Bass" flag at half mast
And as it flutters way up high
It brings a tear to my eye
As I look back and recall
The ghosts of all my "family"
From the Five Bars' wall

Again the language and situations I bring up in this piece are in keeping with the 70s culture of rival gangs. I no way recommend violence, this is just how it was and as opposed to hunting in packs, this was organised gang fights (think West Side Story). The Leasowe fought against Moreton or Ford estate gangs and we fought back against the gangs of Liverpool you saw coming over on ferries with the express intent of doing pitched battles with Seacombe youths. It was what is was.

Dedicated and in appreciation of the Ralph family, Uncle Jim and auntie Hilda, Patrick, Johnaboy my Oppo, Rosemary (Bud) and Sharon. They took me in when I was freezing and hungry into their family abode,111 Church Rd, one of the maisonettes that encircled the (sand) pit.

Also to Jay and Dave Calis, whose mum's veranda we would sing the hits of the day on hot balmy summer nights.

Much love, T U.

The Pit and The Square

The sandpit and the brokey the pump dock and the square
The beautiful stench of the foul Mersey air

The labour club, the five bars
The blue maisonettes
The halcyon days a lad never forgets

The Seacombe Ferry café
The joke box till late
Us strategically planning out campaign of hate

Footy got boring
We wanted to fight
And when the ferry alighted we put that all right

Milk bottles, lump hammers
Stones and bricks
An arsenal full of assorted sticks

We'd fight toe-to-toe
We'd trade blow-for-blow
But we usually legged them, they had nowhere to go

They'd jump back in the river
And swim back to the stage
Get the ferry back home we'd extinguished their rage

Singing on verandas on hot balmy nights
The songs of the charts under fluorescent lights

We'd swim in the Mersey then lie on the prom
With the sun on our backs
Tiddly om pom pom
Wahey!

Or New Brighton baths
What a glorious treat
Collecting pop bottles on the way
To cash in for our sweets

We'd walk to that lido
(Six miles there and back)
But who cares when you're young and you're having the craic?

With your pals, your comrades, your band of brothers
The chosen few
We weren't like the others

The Connyss Club, Cosa, The Joey's, The Float
Growing hairs in strange places
Girls floating your boat

The enemy became friend
Ferries full of girls
Necking sessions on the
Greenhill
Them first teenage thrills

The Stanley, The La-Banque
The Wharf and The Dale
All sadly gone now
Dispersed with the ale

But these memories burn so fierce in my heart
Only my passing will tear us apart

I could name all of the people from The Pit and The Square
Remember all of their faces
The cut of their hair

Some are still with us though scattered afar

Some sadly not
You know who you all are

But alas life goes on and we all drift apart
But we all share that torch that burns fierce in our hearts

Or those far away days of The Pit and The Square
That are in my mind's eye
And will always be there

I remember being honoured to be given the responsibility of preparing and firing up the old cradle in the back room of our two-and-a-box-room abode in 60s Merseyside. No doubt a ritual carried out every morning by kids the length and breadth of the UK.

Fire lighting Duties

Fire Lighting Duty

I hope this piece resonates with those of you of a certain age

Foghorns belching out their mournful honks
Along the mist shrouded
Ominously clouded Mersey

Scraping the ice off the inside
Of your window sill

Walking splintered floors
To don another jersey

Huddled under overcoats
Tops and tails

Making full use of the mattress
Sardine style

As a ships bell sounds
4am and all is well

Time to get up
And light the fire
In a while

Soon I must navigate my way
Across the floor

Dodging them splinters
As I reach the landing light

Just the four steps
From my overcrowded pit
To the bedroom door

Then the safety of the lino
And all feels right!

Then I would clutch hold of the banister
Securing my way down creaking stairs as I carefully
step around each well remembered crack

To the safety of the newel post
At the break of day
and the familiar sight
Of dads auld working "mac"

Then I'd jump across the hallway
Avoiding yet more painful splinters
As I silently made my way to the kitchen door

I'd gather in coal, newspaper & kindling
To warm them frozen winters

Not content until
I'd made our fire roar!

That seems a hundred years ago
When I made that fire glow
and sit by that welcoming hearth
Away from the damp and cold

I never minded being asked
To carry out this daily task
Nor was it a case of doing what I was told

Because we all done our bit back in the day
Never asked for kudos, praise or pay
And central heating will be one helluva godsend when
we're old

Were any of you put on fire lighting duty and were more than pleased because this was a great responsibility taught and passed on to us by our older siblings or parents? What are your memories of being lullabied to sleep and waking to the sounds of ever-present foghorns caught by the wind and carried to your bedroom window on the banks of the Mersey?

I was fortunate enough to start my pub drinking days when the wandering minstrels would come and serenade us with their own mix of acapella skiffle using everything from the spoons to ashtrays, beer trays, harmonicas, Jew's harps etc.

I remember the special guitarist/vocalist Gary Murphy saying to me once, "God Tony, if I could bottle what they have got, I'd be a very content entertainer". Gary you're the tops mate.

In memory of Johnny and Eddie Rutter, Ernie Boyd and Sammy and Kenny McMinn and Bobby Rice, who is still with us, and all the other wandering minstrels far too numerous to mention.

Seacombe FM

Thinking I'm listening to my favourite tunes
But where's the Jew's harp?
The squeezebox?
The spoons?

Sammy McMinn
Bobby Rice
Ernie Boyd

Ya can forget ya Beatles
Beach Boys
And Floyd!

When I first started drinking
Folk said "he's a nutter"
He doesn't want Elvis
He wants Johnny Rutter

The guys that would give
This boy their last shillin'
Get in the queue
Misters Orbison and Dylan!

These are my artistes
They know my life

On the good ship lollipop
Shirley Temple?
Or Millie?

Well whoever said that
Just got to be silly

It was Johnny R
The Cunard Yank

Nice day
That's who I thank

For the music
Not Ringo
Or John, George or Paul

And brother Eddie's "Caruso"
Out-sang them all!

He could shatter the windows
In all of the pubs

Sink all of the ships
And raise all of the subs

They would play with two spoons
Although you'd swear they had ten

Us shouting for encores
Again and again
Off our razor dressed heroes
Real working-class men

IMAGINE Mr Lennon
If you could reach me like them?

Who needed the fab four
And their hysteric din?

We had Rutters and Rice
And Sammy McMinn

These were our voices
This side of the river

They'd pay us for listening!
And always deliver

The pubs have all gone now
Our minstrels as well

But answer me this
Lady GaGa
Adele

Do you think you can better
The tide and the swell

Of our side of the Mersey
You'd have to do well

To beat Johnny and Eddie
Where ever
They'd been

Or young Bobby Rice
And our Sammy McMinn

A quick synopsis of my life from leaving school to travelling the globe for work, and what happened in between.

Much love, T U.

Author's Life

Synopsis of the Author's Life

A quick synopsis of some stand out memories in the authors life.

Roald Dahl and Dan Dare
Pogo dancing
Bright green hair
Mohican style
That 70s flair
Forever gone
Like bubbles into air

London days and Tenerife nights
Australia and long haul flights
The Middle East – now they liked a fight!
Reflecting on my life as yet
It's really been quite bright

These are the things I miss.

Detention centre beatings and borstal nights
Lumpy porridge and jailhouse fights
Months in solitary putting the world to rights

These are the things I'll miss (you read it right)

Working on roofs and living in sin
Nightclub doors and getting filled in
A lot of mornings waking up not knowing where I'd been
These are the things I miss (well some of them ha!)

Them leasow days the best of my life
Marrying the wrong fkin' trouble and strife
I've got to put that all behind me
Coz as Sinatra said 'THAT'S LIFE'
And (like them or not) these are the things I'll miss!

All the girls I've loved before... well maybe only some
The huge regret of not having my girl living in my drum*
But as the man said "you only win some"
These are the things that hurt

(self-inflicted makes the pain tenfold)

My three precious gifts of my grandchildren's laughs

On outings to the cinema the fairground or the baths
God taketh away but he giveth
Seems he's forgave my selfish gaffes

These are the things I'll miss

Of course our lives are chock-a-block
With memories good and bad
Some of them are bitter-sweet
Others just plain sad
But at day's end I can tell myself what's beautiful or pure
bad

And that is a gift I'll miss.

* not bringing up my daughter in my house with her mum
as a family. My own doing makes it harder to bear, but her
mum being happily married to a great guy makes the guilt
a tad easier to bear.

A piece about our daily pilgrimage every day of the summer holidays when I was 14–15 years of age – our misdemeanours whilst in there... naughty! And our triumphant march back home where we would eventually fall into our pits completely exhausted but feeling like kings.

Much love, T U.

School Summer Hols

This will bring back memories a plenty to all of you that converged on new Brighton baths from all over the North West and further afield from the 50s through 80s, and even earlier. This is particularly aimed at the unaccompanied troublesome teenagers of whom there were thousands. We live and we learn, and I'd be the first to give my young teenage and even pre-teen self a good clip round the ear knowing what I do now. However, the rites of passage were what they were and at the time they were the best of days for me and a thousand other little a***holes!

Much love, T.U.

Beach towel, sun cream
Trunks and flippers
A bit OTT for a wee bunch of nippers
Up at seven, we'd get there for nine
We'd commandeer that prom, in a horizontal line

Larkin and laughin'
Some scrapping and laughs
As we made our way up to new Brighton baths

The largest lido in the world
The Mecca of our teenage dreams
Candy floss
Windmills on a stick
Beach balls
And of course ice creams

But no way could we afford any of them
But it didn't stop us looking

Whilst one by one we'd crawl under the turnstiles
While 'old jobsworth' wasn't looking

Once we're in, we're kings of the baths
We'd stand aloft the fountain and shout
"Over 'ere nob head"
To the dilatory attendants
Doing there damndest to launch us back out

But once we were in, we're in for the day
Not a chance of us being ejected
It would have took the eighth army
To chase the Seacombe barmy army
Scurrying home
Heads down DEJECTED!

We knew every trick in the book
And better still tricks that went in it
From grabbing girls for a snog
To hiding in the bog
Or holding our breath under water for minutes
(all true)

We'd stare in envy at the rich kids
Having fun in the outpriced cafe
With Kia-Ora or a frothy espresso
While their Mum and Dad gorged themselves
On endless cream buns
Well before frappuccino or latte

We'd have two keeping Dixie
Whilst us others got bronzed
Under a blistering hot clear blue sky
Then we'd alternate the shifts
Two others keep Dix
After all, who wanted to fry!!

With a bottle of Jusoda or maybe Corona
Or Alpine or maybe Full Swing
We'd take a swig each
Then stroll home down the beach
And in unison in full voice we'd sing

"With big boots and bigger laces
Short cropped hair and smiling faces
Baggy pants and raw red braces
We are the Seacombe BootBoys"

And no matter which way our day had unfurled
We'd go to bed that night
Knowing we were Kings of the World.

Oh, the wonderful cosseted (though tough) days of my childhood, which I'm hoping will resonate with millions up and down the UK in all areas of a certain age.

Much love, T U.

Early Days

Early Days

A trip to your Nan's for a Sunday treat
Garibaldi biscuits and threepence for sweets

A blue and white budgie aloft in a cage
We didn't know it was cruel at that age

Colemans mustard and horseradish sauce
Yer Sunday dinner then home to do chores
Leaving Grandma to watch Peyton Place (of course!)

Washing down paintwork mopping the floors (lino was
befitting and a tickling duster to reach all the flittings)

All of this cleaned with Aunt Sally bleach
It snuffs out the smells other bleaches can't reach

A box car cartie, a hybrid bike
That "I'm a big boy now" change to two wheels from trike

We had bric-a-brac stalls in all the back entries
A lad at each end
Ragamuffin sentries
To hawk all our tat to the front of street gentry!

The girls all adorned in their best daisy chains selling rose
petal water and potions for pains
Pretty girls mucky faces tangled ringlets monied brains!

The five o'clock choir of mums shouting you in
With "Yer tea's on the table" or "where av you been?"

Or "come in the back way" (if you'd a carpet to spoil)
To a big bowl of tripe
Fresh off the boil.

The penny tray
In each corner shop
With a rickety stool to see over the top

Of a counter as high as your back yard wall!
Was it really that high
Or were we just VERY small?

White mice, penny logs
Blackjacks, fruit salads
Mmm this is the favourite part of my ballad!

Talking of favourites
There's downsides too
When my memory goes tired
And I have to leave you

So farewell till next time
And I hope you recalled
The memories as I did
God bless you all.

This one starts in Birkenhead, then over to Liverpool. Shopping then ends up in Wallasey where most of the ol' "gentlemen of the road" who should have been provided for by Mencap off the NHS resided. They would be killed in this frightening age in which we find ourselves, having to fend for themselves but the 50s, 60s and 70s if not a "gentler age", was without doubt a safer one if you found yourself mentally ill, homeless or both. I have been both in the 70s and the 90s and please believe me things got a lot tougher in that relatively short space of 20 years for our homeless... Here's to working toward a gentler age for our descendants.

Merseyside in the 70s (Egerton Bridge)

Throwing ourselves off Egerton bridge
Like a brainwashed slice of lemmings
Then the ferry and the bus to Walton road (Walton)
For some skinners or maybe some flemings

Fred Perry, Ben Sherman
Or a nice Jaytex check
And some two inch roar red braces
To hitch up your keks

A nice pair of brogues
Or some smart square toed commoes
Or for the skins that weren't too well off
Some nine hole major domoes

Doc Martins, Blakeys (pronounced blake-ees – steel toe
and heal protectors to make the footwear last longer)
Or a smart pair of nebbs
For the man about town
In the S.E.B.B or the L.E.B.B. or the N.E.B.B.

A skinhead or a suede head
Which was the greater
I liked the ol' feather cut
That came a bit later

The three day week, the power cuts
The country was a mess
(In the 70s)
But no matter how hard life seemed to be
We still knew how to dress!

Then down to the "lamplighter"
Or maybe "the cap"
A bit of Slade or T.Rex
And the girls were all on tap

Then empty the slop trays
From the pubs and the inns
And all traipse round to the "mullers"
To mix the grog
In old bins
The same old faces coming in and out again
They all had mad nicknames
Like "the Fox" or "the Duck" and "the Hen"

And all the old eccentrics
There's nowhere near as many
Like "what about the buses Norman"
Mick the meths
Or kiss a penny!
Or road sweeper Roy
To whom Elvis was God
But if you mentioned the blue sh**e
He'd holler
"F**K YOU YER little SOD!"

"Has anyone seen Stuart?"
Lamented old totty George
Whilst rooting through the bins
To find something on which to gorge

Then you'd shelter from the elements
In a nice warm launderette
And hide away from the Provey woman
When you were knee high in debt

A nice cosy shelter
Like Ricky Harnett's by the park
When folk weren't afraid
To sleep outdoors after dark

And though times have moved on
I can put my hand on heart and say
the mean streets in the 70s
Were a nicer safer place to stay

This reflects in my mind the bygone days of entering our terrace home through the back entry with their cobbled stones (commonly known as jiggers) as our mothers would be cursing the new carpet getting dirty.

Much love, T U.

Back-to-Back Terrace

Back-to-Back Terrace

A sewing box
Usually an old tea caddy
Full of needles
And threads and old broaches

A sugar butty
Twixt lunch and tea
We all lives
As in films
Like Ken Loaches

And the bath water
After the last child emerged
Was as black as the Western approaches!

Or you'd turn on the light
To the arse clenching sight
Of scattered slugs
And scurrying cockroaches

In our back-to-back riverside terrace

A page from The Echo
Where the glass had been smashed
A pair of dark glasses
Where some poor wife had been bashed

But what happens indoors
Stayed indoors

It was what it was

In our back-to-back riverside terrace

Coming in through the back way
We seldom used the front door

So down the jigger
Swerving bin men
And stray cats galore

"Watch ya don't tread any sh**e in
I've just mopped the floor"

In our back-to-back riverside terrace

Hiding in plain sight
When the tally man came

He could see you through the window
But we all knew the game

If you couldn't see them
You couldn't feel shame!

In our back-to-back riverside terrace

The nightly vigil
To the brick outside bog

You could pee in the po
But you'd never drop a log

And be careful not to trip
Over that useless fecking dog

In our back-to-back riverside terrace

Fetching the milk in on winter morns
In your pjs and woolly hat

The sparrows had pecked the lid of the gold top
But we always blamed the cat

That would "meow" (in cat talk)
After a hoof up the arse
"There was no f*****g need for that!"

In our back-to-back riverside terrace

All big families back then
Squeezed in a "two-and-a-box"

First up best dressed
And never any matching socks

The ritual morning glee
Of that comb through your locks

In our back-to-back riverside terrace

A rusciple spoon full of cod liver oil
A nice mustard poultice
To burst that humongous boil
And every day seemed like one big, long toil

In our back-to-back riverside terrace

Now some may look back in fondness
To them gentler, bygone days

Where folk could leave their doors open
And were "set in their ways"

Me? I've never heard such b****cks
The past's a rose-tinted haze

Times were hard
In our riverside terrace!

Anyone over 58 will remember wee Totty George. He would regularly come over to the railings of St Joseph's School at dinner time and as five or six year olds we never knew the poor man was ill, we just thought he was different. Nearly all of this ode is true. Enjoy your day.

Much love, T.U

Ode to Totty George

Way back in my childhood years of school prunes and
custard

Whilst running round St Joseph's yard
Being shouted at and fussed at.

A wee little man named Totty George

Would make his way over the road from Santis Chippy.
He was a gentleman of the road
And in his worn out coat's buttonhole
Sported a dandelion like some worn out washed up hippy

Then blocking a nostril at a time
He'd snot out funky snot and slime
Saying one was vinegar and the other one was salt!

It was the colour of boiled sh**e
And to our little ears delight
He'd proclaim the vinegar was an "exquisite single malt!"

With it dripping down his lips
To condiment his pie and chips.

And whilst gorging with intent
He'd sing out his sad lament
Before whistling shrilly
Then shouting pip pip pip!

"Has anyone seen a little boy named Stuart"
Lamented Totty George
Whilst tears streamed down his glassy-eyed, cherubic face

At this we'd begin to stop to play
And listen whilst he drifted far away
To another time another place.

We'd heard that a long long time ago
When at 4ft10in George ceased to grow
He'd been employed on the Mersey ferry "daffodil".

Smart as paint and proud as punch
Millenia before his snotty lunch
He'd worked as hard as any salty Bill!

Then one stormy evening when the ferry was mid float
Totty was alone at the back of the boat
The dreaded shout "man over board!" went out.

Our hero jumped in to save a little feller
But submerging with "young Stuart", George took a knock
off the propeller.

The life belt went in and both their souls were saved.

Young Stuart fully recovered
And Totty was commended for the maelstrom he had
braved.

His sea legs remained firm
But alas, the propeller's knock had muddled his head
And for years and years "has anybody seen a little boy
named Stuart"
Were the only words he said.

I heard when I grew older, George was beat up and killed.
Whilst sleeping by the bus stops at the ferry
The gang was never bought to book
Not even one name was took
It was such a vile and senseless killing, who would do it?

There are many names that one could have blamed
Jim or Frank or Bill or James.
Or perhaps one of them was a grown up boy named
Stuart?

For all you that were lucky enough to spend their first year of "big school" in the Old Manor Road School, sequestered by St. Marys R.C. College.

Big School

Big School

In the words of the cat
The 70s bard
Who remembers the days on the old school yard?

Tarmac and gravel and traces of coal
Which led to the coal-hole that had a huge gap
Tailor made to tumble down
Whilst battling, mid-scrap!

The toilets on the playground
For a ciggy and a snog
We don't piss in your ashtrays
Don't smoke in our bog!!

The graffiti grapevine
With "Kilroy was 'ere"
Or Degsy loves Angie
And Mr N—in's a queer!

That first day in big school
When we were bullied to dance
(a ritual we ourselves would continue the next year)
And have your heads pushed down the khazi (and flushed)
While some tw*t pulled down your pants!

The 20ft high windows
The pong of floor wax
Whilst the year head (Mr Calvert) is on the "Assembly stage"
Getting down to brass tacks.

The class nominations
From D through to T (dominus regat)
Hope one of the sexy girls sits next to me!

Though they'd never admit it
Most girls thought alike
But if approached would come out with
'Piss off' or "On yer bike".

The luxury of plumbing
On wet cold windy days
Us sat next to hot pipes
Whilst reciting our plays.

"No playtime today class
its torrential outside"
So over highly waxed floors
We'd slip trip and glide!

At the time I was not that much more than a nipper
But big enough to slide tits up
Or we'll "split me kipper" (Owwwwwwww).

Breaking into the art class
Stealing Indian ink
To tattoo our arms with everything
Besides the kitchen sink!

The winding wooden stairs
Up to the headmaster's lair
For six of the best
Bent over a chair.

Or on the tips of your fingers
Yeh right on the end
Then hands under your armpits
Your poor fingers new friends.

We all have different memories
So is it true or old wife's
Were our schooldays
Really the best of our lives?

Dedicated to all that did their first year of big school at St Marys Manor Rd.

Acknowledgements

Sandra Chapman Ford for so generously letting me use her unique and nostalgia infused paintings to illustrate this book.

Also Jim O'Loughlin and his daughter, Charlotte, who gave up many, many hours of their precious time and skills to make this book happen. I thank you, alongside Amanda Dodd, for all your work and time, typing up the original drafts.

And lastly, but most importantly, the myriad of characters and situations without whom this book would not be.

Much love, T U.